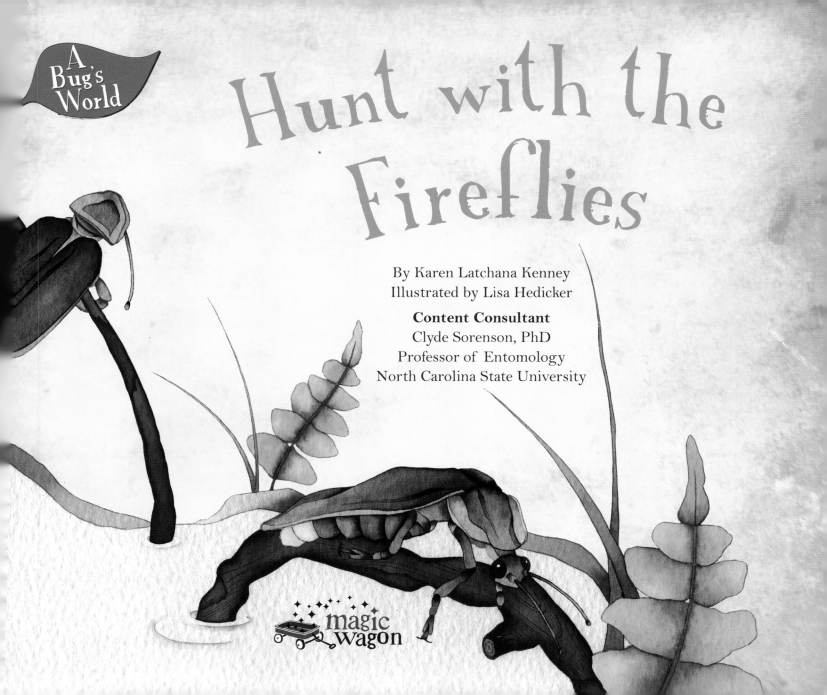

A Bug's World

Hunt with the Fireflies

By Karen Latchana Kenney
Illustrated by Lisa Hedicker

Content Consultant
Clyde Sorenson, PhD
Professor of Entomology
North Carolina State University

magic wagon

visit us at www.abdopublishing.com

Published by Magic Wagon, a division of the ABDO Group, 8000 West 78th Street, Edina, Minnesota 55439.
Copyright © 2011 by Abdo Consulting Group, Inc. International copyrights reserved in all countries. All rights
reserved. No part of this book may be reproduced in any form without written permission from the publisher.

Looking Glass Library™ is a trademark and logo of Magic Wagon.

Printed in the United States of America, North Mankato, Minnesota.
042010
092010

 THIS BOOK CONTAINS AT LEAST 10% RECYCLED MATERIALS.

Text by Karen Latchana Kenney
Illustrations by Lisa Hedicker
Edited by Amy Van Zee
Interior layout and design by Becky Daum
Cover design by Craig Hinton

Library of Congress Cataloging-in-Publication Data
Kenney, Karen Latchana.
 Hunt with the fireflies / by Karen Latchana Kenney ; illustrated by Lisa Hedicker.
    p. cm. — (A bug's world)
 Includes bibliographical references and index.
 ISBN 978-1-60270-787-0
 1. Fireflies—Juvenile literature. I. Hedicker, Lisa, 1984- , ill. II. Title.
 QL596.L28K46 2011
  595.76'44—dc22
                      2009052916

Table of Contents

Blinking Bugs

Blink, blink, blink. Fireflies are making their own light. Their blinking bodies float and dance through the air.

4

Fireflies live all over the world, especially in warm, wet places. The banks of rivers and streams make good firefly homes.

Fireflies are beetles. About 2,000 kinds of fireflies live on Earth.

Growing Fireflies

It is late summer. A female firefly is laying her eggs in the ground. The tiny, round eggs glow.

A few weeks later, larvae hatch. These creatures do not have wings. They stay underground as they grow.

The larvae are very hungry. They are fierce hunters. They eat small bugs, worms, slugs, and snails. Sometimes the larvae work together to capture their prey.

When it has caught a bug, a larva puts a poison into it. The bug's insides become liquid. The larva has no teeth. Now, it can drink its meal. The bug is left as an empty shell.

The larva's body is growing, but its skin is not. The creature breaks out of its old skin. This is called molting.

New, bigger skin is underneath. A larva molts several times over many months.

A firefly spends most of its life
as a larva. Some fireflies stay
as larvae for a year or more.

The larva is ready to change again. It makes a cell around itself in damp soil. The cell is like a little room for the larva to grow in.

Its body turns white. It is now a pupa. The pupa continues to grow and change. After a few weeks, its skin breaks open again. Out comes an adult firefly. Its skin is pale and soft, but it will harden and darken.

Seeing and Flying

If the bug is female, it will have short wings, or none at all. Many females look like larvae. If it is male, it has full wings. Adult fireflies have compound eyes. They help the fireflies sense moving things.

Once a firefly is an adult, its life is almost over. Most adults live for less than one month. Most adult fireflies do not eat at all. But some eat parts of flowers. As an adult, a firefly's main purpose is to mate so that females can lay eggs.

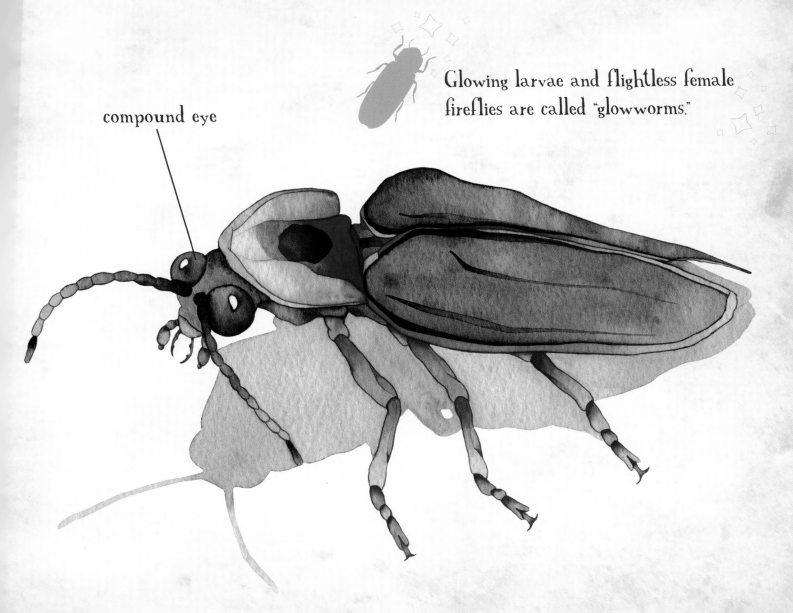

compound eye

Glowing larvae and flightless female fireflies are called "glowworms."

Firefly Light

During the day, adult fireflies rest in the shade. At night, they come out to mate. Blinking helps fireflies find mates. When fireflies blink, it is a way of talking to other fireflies. Each kind of firefly blinks in its own pattern. The pattern helps a male firefly find a female of the same kind. The light guides the fireflies in the dark.

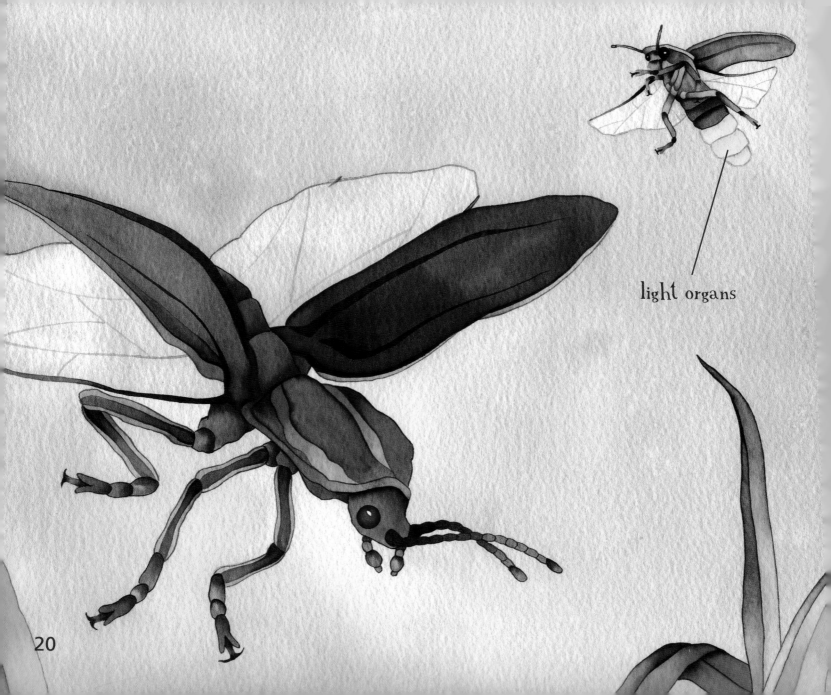

light organs

To make light, fireflies have special body parts called light organs. When a firefly breathes, air mixes with a liquid in its body. This makes light in the light organs. This light can be green, yellow, or orange.

Fireflies do not breathe through their mouths. Instead, they breathe through tiny holes in their abdomens.

To find a mate, a male firefly blinks as he flies. A female is on the ground. She blinks back to the male. Then the male flies down to meet her.

The male has two sets of wings. The front set is a cover to protect the flying wings underneath. Most beetles have hard front wings. But a firefly's front wings are soft, like leather. These front wings lift up. Then the thin, back wings lift the firefly into the air.

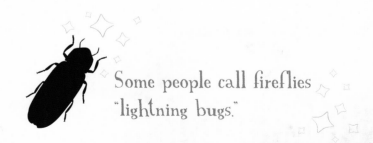

Some people call fireflies "lightning bugs."

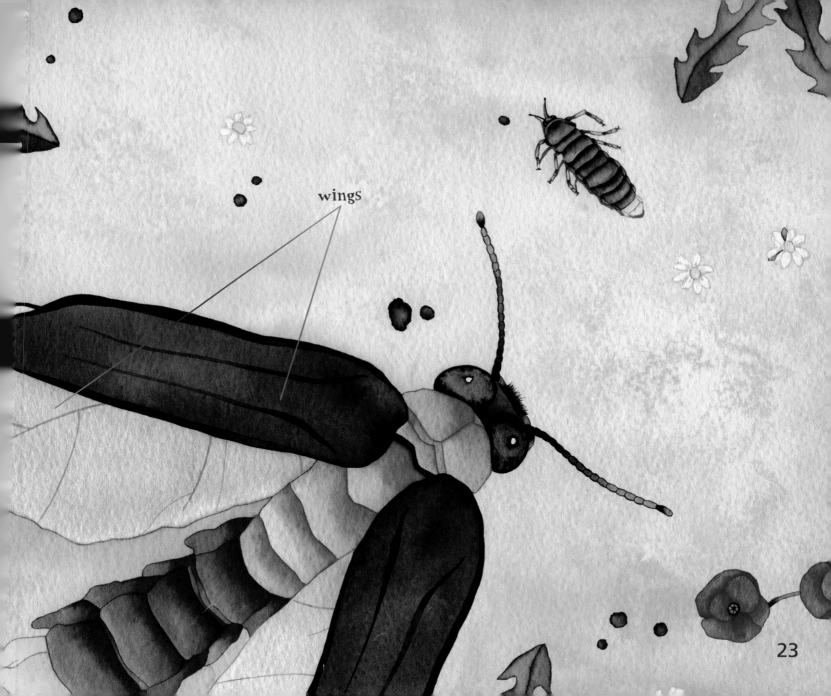

wings

23

Female Hunters

One kind of female firefly eats male fireflies of another type. She pretends to be another kind of firefly by flashing the pattern of another kind. When a male of the other kind flies down to meet her, she eats him!

The bodies of male fireflies contain a helpful chemical. After the female eats the male, this chemical helps her keep predators away.

New Lives

The summer is nearing its end. Fireflies continue to mate. The females lay eggs in the ground. The eggs will hatch. For many months, the larvae will hunt. They will grow and change. Early next summer, new fireflies will begin their lives.

A Firefly's Body

A firefly's body has three main parts: the head, the thorax, and the abdomen. A hard shell on the outside of the firefly's soft body protects it like a suit of armor.

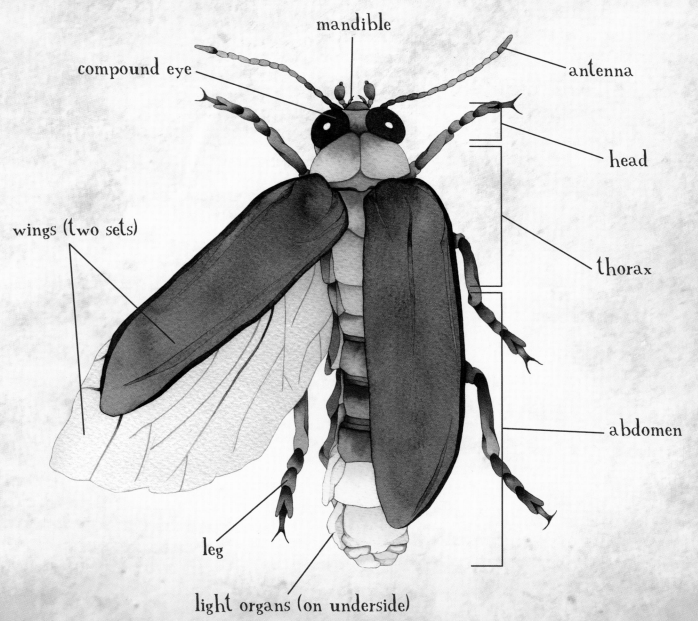

mandible

compound eye

antenna

head

thorax

wings (two sets)

abdomen

leg

light organs (on underside)

29

A Closer Look

Glowing Light

What you will need:

- a glow stick
- a flashlight
- notebook paper
- a pencil

A firefly's light is different from the kind of light that comes from light bulbs. A glow stick makes light in a way that is like a firefly's light.

Turn on the flashlight. Set it next to the glow stick. Draw a line down the middle of a piece of paper. Write "Glow Stick" at the top of one side. Write "Flashlight" at the top of the other side. Look at and feel the light from the glow stick and the flashlight. On your paper, write what you see and feel about each light.

Here are some questions to get you started:

- What is the same? What is different?
- What color is the light?
- How hot is the light?
- How far does the light shine?

Firefly Facts

- An adult firefly is about **1** inch (**2.5** cm) long.
- Some kinds of firefly larvae live in the water. They have special breathing parts like fish.

Glossary

abdomen—the back part of an insect's body.

compound eye—an eye made up of thousands of lenses, with each one taking in a piece of an image.

glowworm—a glowing firefly larva or an adult female firefly that cannot fly.

light organs—the parts on a firefly's body that glow with light.

molt—to break out of a layer of skin so that new, bigger skin can grow.

poison—a harmful substance.

thorax—the middle part of an insect's body.

On the Web

To learn more about fireflies, visit ABDO Group online at **www.abdopublishing.com**. Web sites about fireflies are featured on our Book Links page. These links are routinely monitored and updated to provide the most current information available.

Index